SERIOUSLY

SILLY SIGNS

SILLY SIGNS

WOEFUL WARNINGS, MAD MESSAGES AND DIRECTIONS FOR DISASTER

ARCTURUS

ARCTURUS

This edition published in 2015 by Arcturus Publishing Limited
26/27 Bickels Yard, 151–153 Bermondsey Street,
London SE1 3HA

ISBN: 978-1-78404-513-5
AD004453UK

Printed in China

Where would we be without signposts? Well, we wouldn't know, would we? But, as the contents of this book clearly illustrate, some signs leave us more confused than when we started. Take the road junction with a stop sign at every entrance: who makes the first move? Or the sign that appears to be warning us to beware of corgis. Really?

Wherever you go in the world, you're bound to find a sign or two that make you chortle. A double entendre, a translation faux pas... wherever people try to make things clearer, you'll often find they achieve the very opposite.

So enjoy this collection of *Seriously Silly Signs* and if you find yourself lost, don't blame us – we're only doing what we're told...

The revolution began one quiet Thursday afternoon...

Those Germans – they'll make a game of anything.

Bet the twinning committee meetings are a riot!

Hmm... wrong side of the road, mate.

... leaving the sign-makers with time on their hands.

You're gonna need much bigger binoculars!

As the old saying goes.

But there is an ointment you can get for them.

Tomorrow – go crazy!

And that's an order!

Don't feed the birds.

Whatever you do, STOP!!

Yoo hat bean warend...

He's actually a lovely guy once you get to know him.

They need taking down a peg or two.

Some people just won't take 'No Entry' for an answer.

Don't know about soft shoulder, but this pole sure hits the spot!

You pays your money and you takes your choice.

In case you were thinking about it!

At least they're honest....

It's an easy misteak to maek.

You wait all day for a bup, then two come along...

Security cuts hit Buckingham Palace.

The toilet attendant used to work in advertising.

It's best not to fall out with your sign-writer before opening night...

Ssshh! Don't tell anyone!

Obviously, the scenic route!

Motorway regulations in Denmark are very strict.

Enter at your peril.

Grass is napping,please don't disturb

When does it wake up?

Women's Lib claims another strategic victory.

Some schools will stop at nothing to boost funds.

Quick, he's heading this way!

Lettuce and Pickle are four and five miles respectively.

Traveler from to get into by bus

Some important information seems to be missing...

Frankly, they're welcome to it!

It's the grey ones you've got to watch out for.

None of your bona fide rubbish here!

Erm... how about we skip the forest trek?

Just add tequila!

Spoiler alert!

*It's actually bigger than that.

What happens when sign-writers lose at Scrabble.

The petty feud between day and night managers reaches a new low.

Like you'd want to...

卫生是最重要的
Sanity is the most important

I've half a mind to agree with you.

Might as well turn around now and go home!

Basically, you're stuck here.

That's what they all say.

Day 1 of the Annual Paranoiacs Convention.

For the Wight Food Market, try next door.

ห้ามจอดวันคี่
ODD DAYS

Aren't they just!

Darned control freaks!

But they're so funny!

Crossing rather slowly, I'd imagine.

Nesting where exactly?!

Always worth a giggle.

Doh, you got me!

This'll keep you on your toes.

Excellent! Can we get one for washing the car?

As if you needed directions, you little devil you!

当心滑跌
DON'T FALL DOWN

It may seem obvious, but some people need to be told.

Yep, you're on your own now, folks.

Try saying that after a few beers!

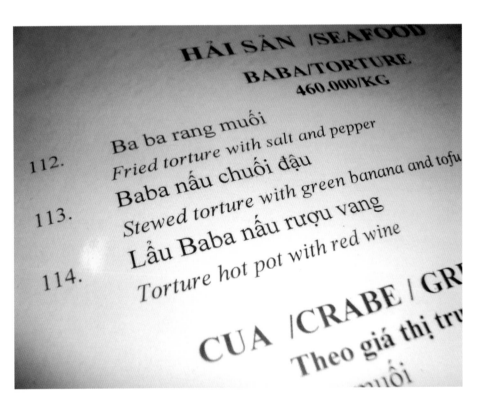

Mad Menu 1: choose your own torture.

round rice noodle

鮮薑肉湯米線

roasted soy duck
egg noodles, crispy shallot, onion, lemon basil and gr

醬汁燒鴨腿湯蛋麵

king prawn *'being blown out of proportion'*
with vermicelli in soup

'大塊頭' 大頭蝦暖暖湯檬粉

lobster-lobster vermicelli in soup
obster and pungent lobster soup

大大龍蝦 · 暖暖湯檬

etnamese sausage
nd rice noodle

Mad Menu 2: it's really a very small shrimp.

NO DOGS ALLOWED

EXCEPT GUIDE DOGS

NO EXCEPTIONS

Are you absolutely sure about that?

You wouldn't believe what goes on around here.

Q.E.D.

Well, what else is it for?

And don't think we won't know if you do.

All his own work.

If you can find it...

Let's just hope he doesn't have his car keys.

Yeah, you're laughing now...

Tenue correcte exigée
dans tout le centre-bourg
_____
Correct vestimentary behaviour
required in all the center bonough

Something lost in translation, je crois.

请勿上下车

NO GEFFWG ON OR OFF PLEASE

If was the edifor's day ott.

Who needs aqua parks?

尊敬的客人：

此花瓶内装流沙, 请不要随意触动, 否则造型会被破坏。

谢谢合作！

Dear guests :

This vase contains quicksand. In order to keep its original shape, Please keep away from it.

Thanks for your cooperation!

There's a perfectly simple explanation for all those missing guests...

Oh, very funny, I'm sure...

Why not?

There's no end to what chickens can do.

Always check the small print.

Let's hope they never have to evacuate.

Wow, that is slow!

Yeah, typical. They never stick at anything, those blind drivers.

WARNING

Gorillas occasionally throw things

And giraffes are prone to bursts of petulance.

One careful owner, low silage.

Star Wars fans would be funny if they could spell...

When you've finished laughing out loud, call 911.

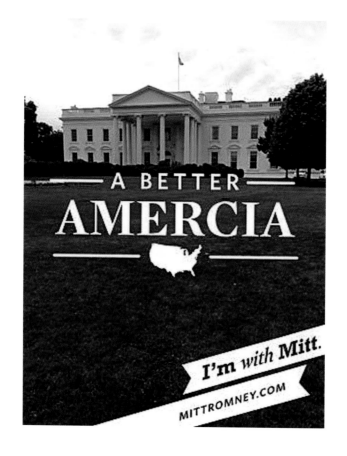

That's a pretty radical proposal, Mitt.

They're still waiting for that phone to ring.

Where nobody is to blame.

We're calling the cops now...

There are some that have been in there for thousands of years.

No turning the other cheek.

Well, it is French.

Please make your fall as spectacular as possible.

The sign that caused a boom in peak hours traffic.

Yes, but it's not much good to me now, is it?

Who are they trying to kid?

On Fridays, just for a laugh they swap the signs over at the zoo.

As epitaphs go, it was short and to the point.

And they said that Funk would never die.

What are you waiting for...?

Welsh point of entry into the virtual world.

If only life was that simple.

I think we get the message.

Where mathematics becomes irrelevant.

And settle back with a long drink as you watch her using it.

Who's going to believe that?!

That's a mighty big groin.

Whose advice will be, "Don't touch any of the crocodiles, stupid!"

SINGLETON SHOWGROUND

AUSTRALIAN WIFE CARRYING TITLES

SATURDAY 27 MARCH

WORLD HUSBAND DRAGGING TITLES
UTE MUSTER

www.countryfest.com.au

Keeping marriage fresh Down Under.

Succinct sign writing at its brilliant best.

Expect delays.

Try not to look... both ways.

What wall?

And they said romance was dead...

How do they know?

At least do it when we're around to chase you off!

Man-eating hedge!

Credits

We have made every effort to contact the copyright holders for the images used in this book. In a few cases we have been unable to do so, but we will be very happy to credit them in future editions.

Cover: Andrew Writer, Corbis, Kevin Ryan, Melinda van den Brink Photography

Adam Main: 6. Alamy: 122. Alex: 118. Andrea Szakos: 81. Andrew Grieve: 113. Andrew Magill: 12. Andy Reed: 80. angrylambie1: 16. adrigu: 102. bert knottenbeld: 115. Brian: 83. Brian Toner: 8. Brian Wolfe: 123. Bridget Coila: 51. bob watt: 10. brett jordan: 95. BuildArk: 111. Charles O'Rear: 19. Chris: 110. Chris Radley: 67. Chris Taylor: 108. Corbis: 22, 41, 66, 77, 105, 112. daryl_mitchell: 49. David: 55. Denise Chan: 71. Dennis Cookson: 125. Dietmar May: 62. domhnallw: 36. Duncan Cumming, flickr.com/duncan/: 37. epistrofie: 52. Francis Curran, copyright www.caughtoutside.com: 25. Gavin White: 70. Getty: 11, 32, 35, 53, 58, 96.

Jack Davison: 39. Jailyn Mayrant: 116. Jake Good: 46. James Shuttleworth: 50. Janet Schowengerdt: 90. Jennifer: 54. Jimapore: 82. Jesseca Keppler: 86. John Morris: 73. Jonas Merian: 84. Jonathan Stilts: 61. Josefine Stenudd: 28. jrb_emeraldo: 99. Karen Apricot: 18. Karl Cranswick: 63. Katie Hasenyager: 117. Kevin Stanchfield: 121. Kicki Holmen: 60, 91. ladybugsnleopards: 13. Lana Williams: 93. Linda Turner: 97. Luciana Taylor-Clark: 98. marcmo: 31. Matt McGee: 127. meltedplastic: 56, 126. Mary Frances Cappiello: 15. Michael Bielitza: 17. Miss Shari: 65. moose on the move: 26. munksynz: 43. Nathan Bush: 47. Norman: 87. palo: 79. Peat Bakke: 38. Paul Hart: 101. peggydavis: 9. Phoebe: 69. piX dust: 92. Press Association Images: 27 (Ben Birchall/PA Wire). Quinn Dombrowski: 94. randomtruth: 44. Rex Features: 21, 42, 68, 74, 78, 107, 119. Ryan Feeley: 29. sallyrango: 20. simon: 104. skittledog: 124. slworking2: 48. Stephanie Steele: 30. Steve Juvetson: 34. Steve Rosenblum: 7. susyr22: 24. Traveller 33a: 64. Tobias C Jensen: 59.

Tracy Moniz: 14. Tom Perry: 45. Tony Worrall Foto: 23, 120. W10: 72. Waldopepper: 103. WordShore: 89, 100. Zach: 85.